LEAVING BLUE MOUNTAINS

Impermanence Press
611 Mar Vista
Los Osos, CA 93402

Kevin Hull can be reached at whEditor@hotmail.com. Books may be
ordered at Booksurge.com and Amazon.com.

Acknowledgments: Appalachian Heritage; Hummingbird; Lilliput; Modern
Haiku; Hobo (Australia); Dasoku; Forpoetry.com; South by Southeast;
Cicada; Sister's Today and Coalesce Press.

ISBN 1-58898-813-9

LEAVING BLUE MOUNTAINS

Kevin Hull

2002

LEAVING BLUE MOUNTAINS

CONTENTS

I
THIS FLOATING PAGEANTRY

II
STILL LIGHT, STILL SHADOW

III
THE BREATH OF THINGS LIGHTLY BORNE

*for that spark of reality manifested as . . .
beloved, child, friend*

The real endures, the unreal passes away.

Upanishad

I
THIS FLOATING PAGEANTRY

A GEOGRAPHICAL SOLUTION

It does make a difference;
distance can be a blur or a star.
The air kisses us in the ways of a lover,
sharp teeth or wet caresses, and sounds
drift upon the currents like a poem in translation.
Any era or spirit; architecture of fragrance.
Orange blossoms, lemon blossoms,
a river of sun.
Yo amo tu espiritu, says the traveler
to his arrival: wherever I find my heart,
I find my answer.
Yo amo tu espiritu . . .
and from the reservoir of his life
unfold new roads of walking,
new vistas of sight.

LOST HILLS

A man's emptiness cannot be filled by television,
friends, drugs, dissipation or politics. It haunts him,
year after year, like the heart of the hills he loves.

Those hills are questions: How deep are your feelings?
Have you found your God? A steady wind piling sand
on sand to reach the destined namelessness.

His life hides in the silence of the hills,
the horizon sealed as a vision of God.
Beauty was made for him; he is a blood relation.

He grows into his death,
and leaves with his questions intact—
the very act of asking a kind of answer.

THE CONCH

for Cody

I tell him an ocean
dreams inside this tiny spiral,
that beneath these spiny ridges
are the currents of unmeasured grace –
music and light unfolding,
returning through a single breath
to a language of harmony and praise.

"No, dad," he says. "That's not it.
It's only the wind and the waves."

DREAM POEM

Once in a dream
a poem formed in perfect harmony
of heart and mind, each word
in its place,
each phrase conforming precisely
to its content, resonant
with mystery
and meaning;

as if it had been composed
by a natural man,
who lived, in comprehension,
a natural life.
On waking, that world
slowly dissolved
into the clarity of another sleep,

my feet planted on earth,
my head in my hands.
It was my best work.

As always, beyond me.

HUNGER

for Grandpa

A gallon jug of homebrew
has soured in the cobwebs
under the ancient bed.
A banjo lies busted in the loft.

Late at night he leaves the tomb
and returns to a shattered world,
humming *Wildwood Flower*—
cherries falling in the rain.

"Seems like it's all been a dream,"
he whispered. And was gone.
Who can say what he embraced?

Mother stood alone
beside his plot of ground,
calling down one miraculous rose,
waiting in the charity of her silence
for the blossom to fall.
Who can say?

Even now he crosses the fields,
singing to himself
an anonymous world in repose.

FATHERS AND SONS

A man staggers into the woods alone,
remembering a woman's silent demand
to a world that could not help her.
Her gift will be his distance.

A child is born
and finds two eyes looking back—
one bright spot to center the blur.
A thousand years in search of this silence.

Damp morning, I find him
working on a bridge. His forehead is intent,
his hands firmly gathering.
All around us: the singing of birds,
the scent of honeysuckle and pine,
a dogwood in flower.

He turns and sees me,
jumps out of the footing,
and reaches to shake my hand:
two men in the cold morning light.

Years slide by with hardly a thought.
The hair turns white, curls in the ear.
And the old poet who neglected to write
passes the night thinking
of the son he never had.

THE CONTRARY

for Ben

He draws left-handed alien figures
who walk backwards whispering,
"I have eaten the moon."
He asks for the mustard
when he wants, first of all,
a pillow for his teeth.
His hand moves always in reverse,
and when silent his solitude is palpable,
bathed in a musical light.
I do not truly know him,
he is God's child.

ELEGY

Inevitable to see you here at last,
lowered against your will into this window-less vault.
Or did you in the end offer yourself
to that greatness you spent so much resisting?
Irrevocably split, you of eighty-eight years,
woman of the mountain field, laborer
grown weary toward the mystery of death—
what have you to do with this ritual
or these words?

May your vision trace a new dimension,
silence joined with all the songs of your being,
the unspeakable reconciled.

AS IF

for LaDan Axdahl

I am writing, as if she were gone.
As if she could die to us.

Either we are real or we are lost,
no matter how long we reside here,
or how briefly we grace the dream.
In any case, we are transients, all.

One day the story concludes.
No happy ending, I suspect, nor sad—
for us there must be something unknown
and unknowable, beyond the naming,
real.

Who are we then,
if not the essence of the other?
One life, many dreams.
To what do we identify? To whom?

We wanted to solve the problem of existence;
and to love.

I was her *asaw*, her cane, she joked,
teaching me a little Farsi, as we laughed,
navigating the flagstones.

I wish she had waited.
I wanted to sit with her again,
meditating, hand in hand, beside her wheelchair.
She was alone in the awakening.
Her soul was ready, her soul was ready.

As if we are not our souls.
As if we have identified with something else.
As if there were something else.

In the end nothing mattered.
We were left bereft, foolish with our torn maps
to eternity, our unreliable knowledge, and our searching.

One must study life directly.
Inside the darkness, one's own darkness,
one must have the determination to find the light,
one's own light.
Thus one is qualified to himself,
to speak to himself and of himself,
and if anyone is interested,
to another.

But this cannot qualify another.
And so I say her face, gracious and kind
in the face of crushing fate, taught me more
about courage and human nobility
than all the scriptures and philosophies of the world.

Gradually disfigured by the creeping paralysis,
her eyes never changed, and shone
with grace and beauty.

This was her world.
She inhabited it more than I.
She was a friend while I remained a stranger.

Near the end,
she sat in her immobility,
a silent teacher, teaching
the secret of surrender.

I suggested she fly toward infinity
with purpose and a smile.
She smiled, forever gracious.

I would lift her into bed,
arrange the pillows, and gather her necessary items—
the plastic water bottle, her notepad and pen,
the telephone—and I would tiptoe back
to my walking world, leaving her alone
in the darkness.

It happened that she would slip
into a position of discomfort
and, unwilling to wake me at 3 a.m.,
suffer the night without sleep,
saturated in tears of helplessness.

What is this crystal of consciousness,
the flower of a person, and the seeking?
Simple children's dreams. . .

There are just so many green afternoons.
Hanging pictures in her new condo, her new home.
There, and *there* . . .
Not that one, that one . . .
testing my patience in the sweet absurdity of minutia.
Everything an art.
Her home: at last to be at home.

And the storm comes wrecking our makeshift worlds,
birthing philosophy from the bowels of dubious fate.
Give unto God . . . Yes, and do not love too intensely.

Touch lightly like one who is not really sure
of her existence, and be gone.
No more need for these decorative lies:
the lies we tell each other;
the lies we tell ourselves:
that we are *living* the life that can't be lived;
that we are *doing* what can't be done.

Arrange the furniture; answer your email.
Kiss your sister goodnight.
One day we will return to the matrix.
Who is this beneath the blue sky,
neither dead or alive, but alone?

I know my words are as ineffectual
as the doctors who sent her home to die.
But God, they say, is listening.
I want him to listen.
This too, after all, is his voice . . .
or no voice at all.

What have I learned by loss?
What have I learned?

You have broken my heart, Father.
For no one else could help.

No one else could hear.

You put poetry in me like pills of pain
I could not swallow.

I spit out this music and leave it behind—
a placebo to satisfy the ignorance?
No, not even that.

But I have seen something in this life;
how one thing consumes another's gift
and thereby releases that other
of a burden . . . the burden of the gift.

Maybe we too will be released
from all that is pressing us to be who we are
and who we are not.

One day, perhaps, the mystery
will release us from the burden of its gift—
this homelessness—

and we will achieve a freedom beyond naming.

My dear friend.

WINTER MOODS

Frosty morning . . .
a dog barks in the distance.
I am alone and yet
someone sits sipping his tea,
in the baseless assumption
of a particular identity.

The sad facts of existence:
so seldom does life intervene.

I read bits and pieces from old notebooks,
amazed that I can write at all.

Those I love are walking in the snow.
The mail is late. I wait impatiently
for news that I exist, that I am loved.
They are walking in the snow
beneath the blossoming trees.

What is this place, this person, this poetry?

In my latest dream, it is Spring,
and she is a tiny baby-child again.
I cradle her in my arms, laughing;
and as we leave the playground,
she squirms and says,
"I want to eat the berries in the snow!"

CESAR VALLEJO WALKS
THE STREETS OF PARIS

Cesar Vallejo saw death moving
in the sad-eyed mongrel graces,
flaring behind the stone irises,
and sinking into the resounding sea.

He knew the future would prove his words,
as humanity continued to build gaudy monuments
to utter nonsense, and the unlived unspoken truth,
handcuffed between ambition and dread,
pulled them down into the black waters.

Cesar Vallejo knew we were dead,
and tried to sing us back to life . . .
walking the streets of Paris in the rain,
a ragged beggar asking door to door:
Have you seen life, can you spare a crumb,
is there a kind word hidden in your breast,
a smile struggling to overcome?

A poet approaches a door on a rainy morning,
he staggers and stutters, and, finally, he falls.
They bury him in the earth, and speak sacred words
over his dream of a life. And then they turn
and carry their deaths home to supper.

A CONVERSATION

Our words haunted the natural world,
bouncing across ambition's immaculate table.
He scoffed and a gravestone rose, unadorned,
out of nothingness like a tongue.
"Will you lose this chance, man,
for the sake of poetry? Get with it!"
Then I said: "Will you deny the unknown
for the simple pleasures of certainty?
Your cup may hold any elixir or silence,
breath of a new song, unalterable,
burning edges of dream."
He just laughed.

FOR MIRA

Digging in the sand, we come upon a stick
shaped like a man. Later we will throw it into the sea.
Imagine the sandpiper's skeleton, only an insinuation
of flight—bone and material for making bone.

We walk low-tide across the mussel-crowded rocks,
light and sound dragging the day along.
Noise settles in. We amble around,
dumb and proud.

When I began this poem,
I didn't know how forces would blend
in proportion to the breadth of your steps,
our songs nourishing another life
newly arrived like a child.

The dunes shift and groan in the wind,
forming eccentric shapes that bend and flow.
Sometimes, too, the child between us
forms almost a likeness of itself—
In His own image—and we listen,
behind the thin veneer of memory,
to the music playing in our souls.

Daughter, I wish you grace
to find the one whose trail your small steps
already begin to trace, one to keep you company
where I must stay behind, traveling among the things
that can't be said.

SELF-MADE MAN

in memoriam: Willard J. Ingram

He disappeared one typical morning,
complete as a scar, a mere man,
absurd as the rest of us,
his life a curious riddle.

His life, too, was the life and death of God,
his deeds as unexpected as his love;
a mere man equal to the sum
of the insoluble.

A man dies anonymous as a breeze
after a twelve hour battle for breath
in which, in the end, his lungs turn to liquid
and pour out his gaping mouth
an untranslatable scripture.

His eyes did not see anything worth seeing;
sight was no longer an ally, if ever it was,
his heart clearly alone in spite
of protestations to the contrary.

God was taking him now,
in spite of the tears, in spite of all the work
left pending, in His own way.

The little man, reduced to hollow-eyed frailty,
had just honored the *moment*
for which he had been born,

the Self wishing to be itself again, one life,
returned from desperate multiplicity.

THE INHERITANCE

You surfaced like morning,
offering annunciation in a spirit of belief . . .
and I groped into your lives,
fearful and possessed by the grief
and grace of this elliptic orbit.

I watched, unnoticed,
as you began your devotional songs,
eyes focused on nothing;
as if some part of you
suddenly understood
all that was needed to seize a world,
all that was not your own.

From that day,
your eyes were milky
with an old sorrow.

I remember you most as babies,
floating like Buddha in your new skin,
each of you, a personality
seasoned by the infinite.
And in your eyes the joy
of a thousand suns, the dissolution.

Dear children:
What will I leave you?
An old guitar, boxes bloated with memory,
some worn-out shoes? Maybe a million
dollars or a book, who knows?

What my father could give,
I too will offer: all the good and evil
of our unintended ignorance,
and this—my song of faith,
surrendered freely.

LUNCH AT DENNY'S

Notches on the scale of insanity and reason,
conscious, unconscious, alive, dead—
is a root beer ever just a root beer?

Sitting in a fog of voices, faces like totems, a haunting
of faces in a circle of black magic and tender love.
Pretending to be alive. Pretending I am not
embarrassed to be here, in this room,
in this thin skin.

One of the boys, one eye opening seas.
But vision has deranged me. Lack of vision
has castrated me. A crazy philosophical eunuch,
I go eating, I go hunting—Satori!

Yes, and her ankles are swollen pitiably,
broken veins blurred beneath the thin hosiery.
It feels unreal, this looking.
Her knees are gnarled in folds of fat—
in the dull pain we have forgotten where we are.

She navigates the floor, the coffee pot,
a persistent struggler frightened at the sound
of a beating heart, like the rest of us,
doing what she has to do—
stubborn as dust.

Her tears are poised on the precipice of a face,
obvious as the fork she has forgotten to bring.
We will not let her jump . . . Counting the moments,
the years—suddenly a thin smile, gracious
and self-conscious, her eyes angelic and confused
in the subconscious need of Being, of finding oneself
being somewhere. A kind of prayer, a singular moment,
the last moment, where our names are written in mist and blood.

You have never seen anyone and you will not see me.
Unspoken hope willing this unwilling meat,
an apron of questions. We might have existed once,
but the movie is winding down. The gestures are only gestures, the coin
behind them abandoned like a plea.
Having forgotten my root beer she has brought me two;

one, the sweet cold liquid I had desired; the second,
a compensatory metaphysical soft drink,
a discourse, a proof.

A sense of ridiculous triumph breaks my dumb heart once more,
another dubious victory, another dubious reward.

TRAVELER

Having arrived, freezing, at the abandoned shack,
the solitary traveler scanned the room with a practical
eye: Nothing. The fireplace clean as ash. He emptied
his pockets: an unpaid bill which weighed on his
conscience, a letter from an old friend, never answered,
a child's drawing, his beloved's new address, she who
had abandoned him, and a thick wad of poems, recently
composed. He found, too, a dog-eared book of matches,
just a single match remaining.

His love shone with a warmth beyond words,
and it was a sweet flame for as long as it lasted.

ZERO

i was a white zero
left to my walker and my fat

a black zero taught me manners
mother slept days and slowly lost her mind

she didn't realize that being a zero was a good thing
she wanted to be filled up

and have many things around her
to justify her great size

my daddy was a zero and i loved him all the more for it

that was long ago
in the circle's thin decline

before the revolutions burned us up
and we forgot where to put our eyes

we used words all the time
but nobody understood anything anyone said

we forgot we were the same
circle empty blazing with energy

so strong no body could contain us

but we were clever—
fighting for king of the hill

i groped away
distance filled my orbit

i was a circle circling myself—

purple mountains and orange flowers
clear streams and monarch butterflies

red spires and singing canyons
roads   roads   roads

beercans—razors—toilet seats in strange towns
names like shamrock or amarillo

names like arkadelphia or pecos
names like alamagordo or lordsburg

i looked into those names
and followed myself around the hemisphere—

the desert whispered night's infinite seductions,
softly, sensuous, beyond every thing

some zeros—now become non-zeros—
even named the stars

something hurt inside the circle
other circles had round eyes
with rock walls and box-canyons

i felt strong cold winds swirling
swirling within me—

so hot and cold and alone
the hurt was a climb in the clouds

you will not care to step inside the circle
the perimeter is civilization and hope

the line of brilliance and fame
the rocket launched to the impossible

nothing is vertical nothing is horizontal
not from here to there nor from there to here

nothing is beneath the microscope
in all shapes and sizes   nothing particular—
just us nothings, the no thing
no one can claim—

but the non-zeros claim the world,
the circle they can see from space pictures

they watch their smoke assemble
at the bottom of the sphere
and rip holes into nothing—

they watch the ancient wheel roll upon the circle
tearing away trees and making the frogs angry

what they do then is a linear logical dream,
a felt existence   a kind of unraveling

dark lines scratched into striated clay
baked   half-baked   straight into knowledge—
the thing calling its own name

the zero has no thought for itself
and gives out its round light to horizons
no one can touch
and it never sleeps

i wish mama had named me zero
and realized her zero nature
my blond curls free in the infant breezes

i could have been a real no body—
i could have remembered, and always listened

maybe i could've heard the real music
and never have made such terrible squeals

but i cried, and the other non-zeros cried too,
we all cried and cried—and we embraced,
we built houses with flower boxes and chimneys

fire was power, words were power
we invented money and causes
legend gave us dramatic truth,
our truth deformed into beastly legend

something nearly real—*of our own*
all we ever wanted   our own to keep forever

like a name   a beloved who would obey us
the beginning of the profane and the sacred
that would multiply and multiply and expand us

we built these *lives* for ourselves
from things, funny-faced particular things

we rounded the corner of thought—
sensing something we might not have been
which was the zero's all along

we couldn't remember   we were so far
gone

—forgetting forged words of religion and science
economics and art

we forgot not to eat a world we inhabited,
not the whole thing, not all in one big bite,

and not even in crazy little nibbles
we just ate and ate

zeros are never hungry   of course
the real zero is its own food

why do we stick in our throats
the fateful song, self-destroying, redundant, voice-full, music-less?
why this and that?

praise the zero

it is the understanding you give yourself
as you've lost yourself

as you've discovered your very own
nothing

—unreality winning-losing the nameless found

HORSES OF PARADISE

for my sister, Teresia

My sister loved horses and horses loved her.
Saint Francis loved everything and birds
perched on his shoulders. We attract everything
to ourselves according to our love,
and therein is life's justice and justification.

Horses grow old grazing on green slopes,
sway-back mares or proud stallions put out to stud.
One day our loved ones see us as enigmas or fools,
and perhaps love us in spite of everything.

Perhaps not.

The plum trees are in bloom
with a color and a charm beyond naming.
I think of love's beauty, how it changes
and remains the same—

riding the wind across the meadows of paradise,
bare-back, looking straight into the center of things.

GHOST

What I write on the mirror few will ever see.
Even while alive I was removed from the living.
The clear mountain stream ran through me,
but I couldn't drink.

I stood in life as in death,
watching the energy circle the hollows of its song,
without me.

My desires became their own distance,
tempting me with the pleasures of the body,
as if voice could adorn silence
with the objects of its devotion,
beyond the whispers of appearance and mortality.

I have lived all manner of ignorance,
haunting myself like a dream.

IN OUR WAITING

suffered down to basics
after everything
the best thing

human perception
holding back the flood
in every body the same being

in the center of emptiness
in deepest space, alone,
and within the crumbling walls
and artifacts of dream

the wish
come to chisel identity
in the impersonal sky
where does it go?
this loving this losing?

breaking inside
to another vastness
and nowhere to hide

surrender

we have become perfect,
and perfectly unknowable
we are the mystery

so many mandalas and mantrams
a precipice, a voice calling us to jump

no body   *no mind*   *no expectations*

falling only to rise
in a circle of song

music is the foundation of the world

this melody travels far
each note a perfect sounding

listen

we are what we love,
completely—
how can that ever be lost?

THE BORDER

Burros nap beneath the cottonwoods,
while life itself cries tears of blood.
It is raining in the desert.
Harsh weather in the temples of freedom,
life listening to the silence
of a man judged less than a man
because he hasn't the necessary papers,
dollars or skin, because he hasn't
understood the true import
of the industrial revolution
and still thinks his life is his own.

In the dusty furrows,
rocky river channels, fences cut
for a hundred miles, and mended again,
someone is creeping.
The people sing sad and gentle songs,
wild and hungry songs.
It is snowing distance, cold as a lie.

The horizon speaks death,
eternity expelling stars, moons, songbirds.
A child is born in the arroyo to a face of shadows.
Everyone speaks to God, but few listen,
lost in a fog of sound.

Waiting for the world to go away,
great polluters, great hypocrites,
drink wine from the Napa valley,
while billionaires control the ocean's poetry,
thugs in silk pajamas keeping power in a wall safe.
A beautiful woman looks up from her champagne
and laughs at the moon's wanton halo.

You too can ride the hobby horse of blind ambition,
you too can be a mover and a shaker.
Silver spoons still brush lipless sneers,
real diplomas floating in the cobbler.
This, the age of significant unreason,
computer technicians and genetic engineers
waiting for the mind to catch up.

Old generals handsome in their epaulettes,
prepare speeches for the next lost election,
remembering snatches of stupid movies,
the shine of empty chamber pots,
and sultry mulattos on islands far from home—
man of the people and the pocket—
blessed of amber grain and stars unnamed
after dead gods and cartoon geniuses.

Stars billow in the breezes.
Having made the sacrifice anything goes.
Existence is its own meaning.
I would show them the film they have created
in arrogance and greed, starring phantoms
and dead men lost in dust storms of illusion.
Life itself screams bloody murder and loneliness,
a spotlight whirling in the drain.

I would show them the coming attraction,
with *death* singing *static*.
But we are the poor crowds staggering along
in furrows of forgetfulness and need,
intoxicated by our breathing.
Who are we kidding?
Our poems cannot build a missile,
elect a president, or raise the Dow.

We are the patriots of a land yet formed.
Our future is written in fields of blood,
the happy march to oblivion and the kisses.

CERRO ALTO

for Jason

Clear above the fog and trouble,
we discuss the nature of God, the Mysteries.
I am relieved to find in my son
thoughts of his own.

I say what I believe, and tell him
that I have no real faith in words.
Why then do I write?
Because it isn't the words
but what may come through the words.

Holding forth, I spy the old nemesis:
Identity or annihilation?
Fulfillment or flood?
What kind of consciousness?

The mind wants to know
but the syllables of the heart
pour out silently.

We sit gazing upon folds
that carry, irretrievably,
down to the sea.
A hawk emerges from the brush,
soars below us.

And in us something merges:
doubt and love, fear and joy balanced, as it were,
on a precipice, a cloud, a wave.

CONSTRUCTION WORKER

I became what I had always shunned, by doing nothing.
In doing nothing many obvious things are allowed
to happen, crude fates and facts measured to fit
our accommodating souls. Too dumb to use my brain
for worldly peace and prosperity, I was forced to put
my back into my hungers, the chronic dis-ease
of a man-sized appetite bringing grief and joy
in its pleasures. Everyone called this *Life*,
but I was skeptical. So I set out upon the road.
That suspicious traveler decided to make Art
from his ignorance, and so stumbled into poetry.
What did he seek to say? Just this: *I have a power*
my hands cannot address nor my brain represent.
I will never express it. I am its expression, too primitive,
too savage, and too absurd to be believed, a poor translation,
an indulgence, a dream. However . . . And the human wishes
pile their ashes against the human will.

CROSSING

To step out of one's self,
and not look back. To go on,
as if it were the first day.
No longer to work in fits and starts,
fire and ice vying for our hearts.

Twenty-seven hundred miles from home.
Tired. To the west a gray sky
broken like lace, and behind it,
a thin line of gold streaming into darkness.

Who understands the silent mountain?
The earth aches, and the voice
has nothing to say.

Crossing the prairies of Winter,
I listen to the energy recede toward the tap root,
and think of forests locked in a bubble,
rising and falling in perfect equipoise.

It is cold, and the air is difficult.

I take root in the music.

THE DISTANT ROOM

I am the last to retire. It is I who must
walk among the quiet losses of a day,
minor victories and tiny joys made equal
in the utter elusiveness of it all.

Dolls, face up on the carpet, speechless,
stare at me as I tiptoe through the obvious,
wishing another world for these unsuspecting souls.
Bombs are falling, people are cheering,
and I have the rent to pay.

Brush your teeth and go to bed.
Say your prayers. Everything will be okay.
I'll leave the door ajar. Goodnight sweethearts.

The natural clutter of the day is art at its purest.
It needs no sham artifice to break your heart
or send you into hysterics. I admire the drama
of the day, its spiritual consequences;
willing to laugh yet unable to muster
the enthusiasm.

I am careful not to disturb the dolls
staring up from their lonely suspension,
abandoned for the long dark night.
There is a kind of life in the plastic world.
What we have given to the loveless and the dead
wakes, almost believing, almost touching
the bed of hope on which they, through us, lie.

The room in its pity almost comes alive.
Tomorrow voices and complaints,
laughter and petty squabbles, a cluttered
room of wishes gone awry—God's little toys
going through the motions of skill and madness.

Soon I will begin again my sleepwalking love affair
with conditional truth, an accidental guide
through the corridors which end each day
in the maze of self, no child's father,
no teacher of humankind.

Then the figures will pantomime
in repetitive vagaries the dream of life.

LOVE AND DUTY

The old man remembered his daughter,
that sweet child, now, suddenly, fifty,
and blushed into a gentle
suppression of tears.
It goes quickly, he said.

I thought of my own child then,
something she once said to me
in an outpouring of knowledge and pain.
A simple cry, old as time:
I want something I can keep!

We live for a different answer,
in a question no heart can understand,
our lives passing in a dream.

Our love, too, has its demands:
we who lived captive
must die free.

II
STILL LIGHT, STILL SHADOW

BLUE MOUNTAIN

I began writing while on the road, but everywhere I traveled the old confrontation—the dreamer waking in an unfinished world.

> *my mind wanders*
> *in its grooves—*
> *a flower blooms*

A voice seeks among the debris of many seasons one clear word, well-rooted, a bearer of fruit. Philosophy and Poetry make their vows. Whose voice? Whose regard?

> *I sit writing*
> *in twilight—*
> *soft rain*

We walked along the overgrown road to the broken-down sawmill, looking for trees; found two little oak saplings, a maple, a white pine, what we thought to be a birch, some mountain laurel, and a bush for which no one had a name.
I dug them up and brought them home, a beautiful day in early summer, my favorite season. I thought I had a dream, but in the end I was merely sleeping.

> *torn clouds*
> *among blue mountains*
> *rays aslant on the peaks*

My son tells me about a stationary firefly, glowing from a neighbor's yard. He watches from his upstairs window late at night when I think he's sleeping. He, too, is gauging the immeasurable, building an inner life . . . alone.

a world gone mad,
from shore to shore —
I play catch with my boy

My work is not my possession but a path, overgrown and dark, winding deep into the wood. Some call it poetry, others god. It has all the love a life could need, pursuing, fleeing. And although I cannot see how the work gets done, I hear life singing clearly in all that does and doesn't breathe.

winter moon
another obvious fact
another hidden truth

Why then do I walk on, restless and confused?

STILL LIGHT, STILL SHADOW

form is the shadow
cast by an obstacle
that doesn't exist

the laughing children
a shower of jonquils
on the flowing stream

in every house,
behind every door:
the same person

isolate prairie. . .
in the solitary oak
a riot of crows

learning when to let go—
that cool deep water!

unconcerned . . . tiny
winged crawler crossing my hand
crossing the flower

mind thinks it is somebody
free awareness narrowed down to delusion
emptiness dissembling emptiness

folding the dropcloth
a tiny lizard dashes
into the woodpile

fly in the window
curled on its back in sunlight
a world beyond reach

cat-leap
the firefly
extinguished

neglected garden
a tiny watermelon
among the thin vines

"I" am the barrier
life seeks to overcome
like a river returning
to the sea

first snow . . .
the dark patches
where she rolled

fragrance of woodsmoke . . .
guided by my half-filled tracks
in the moonlit snow

O ant! in such a flood
there are no strangers

prodigal son . . .
showing us his collection
of foreign coins

ahh! this human life . . .
hungry for the glitter—
spittle in moonlight

that night as we dreamed
a stunned possum left drag marks
in the dusty road

even in dense fog
the white heron cannot hide
its perfect silence

ORIGINS

Night birds sing in the anonymous hours,
cool breezes of dark infinity,
old messages for the forces
alive in star and stream . . .
the breath of things in form,
inhaling the formless.

Rising from the silence of listening,
the center untouched by thought,
breathing the given life, already
distant.

Shadows bleed essence,
and substance is a revelation
we are too slow to grasp,
too frail to hold.

And beauty a long thin scar
across the heart that knows.

GOOD INTENTIONS

my good intentions:
opening my hand in the open air—
moth dust

nudging the frog
from the desert of my van—
casually a bird comes
and gulps him down

a frog falls from the great oak
into my open trunk and hides, instinctively,
from my good intentions: the red sun
blossoms upon the singing land.

CASTING WITH THE WIND

for Michael

We walked the drying shores of Santa Margarita Lake,
in the ostensible role of fishermen. It was the first day
of Autumn, hot and dry. The lake was in drought, its
waters concentrated.

> *casting with the wind*
> *vegetal remains remark*
> *the lake's slow descent*

"There's fishing, and there's catching," Michael said,
as if to appease me. But it was obvious which activity
we were doing. And, in truth, I was relieved. What was
I doing here? I'd been a vegetarian for over twenty years.
I had no intention of catching. "But the fish will be
concentrated in the lake's decline." "Yes," I said, "but
it's hot." "Yeah, it's hot," he said. "We'll see." I imagined
the fish asleep deep in the mud. Michael taught me
to cast, and gradually I became more or less proficient.
I enjoyed the motion, without expectation.

> *with an easy toss*
> *I let go of the line—*
> *my mind searching the depths*

I was 'fishing' after all. Why not? I had fished all my life,
for compliments, for sex, at times even for the Absolute.
Why not fish simply for the fishing? We cast and cast our
lines, trying various places, in meditative silence. Cliffs of sparse pine and
sheer stone surrounded the lake, reminding me of photographs I'd seen of
the wild places of China. Suddenly the wind came alive.

the wind riffles the blue waters—
the cast line driven back
limp and obvious

We were the only humans there, except the crow on
the brown stone who thought he was human. He looked
around as if requiring comment. And as you can see, he
got his wish. On the north shore, protected from this
vindictive wind by peaks and trees, we cast our lines
again and again.

we seek to fool
the wise old bass—jerking
the fake frog ever so deftly

The lake is ringed with gelatinous afterlife; the receding
waters concentrate the lake's hidden life, but it is hidden
nonetheless. The waters have descended from the brown
stones, a bowl-like declivity now ringed by newly emergent shoreline.
Beneath the crunch of drying vegetation and crustaceous debris, an
untrustworthy muck. We walk lightly.

nobodies poem,
they laugh in the cool deep—
like an archetype of hunger and sleep

I had fished all my life, unknowing, and on this day of
fishing, free of intent, I caught, unsought and unexpected, a little peace of
mind. For a time, I was simply casting my line over and over with the wind.

no fish, no bait—
whose food are you,
wind?

REASONS FOR NOT KILLING

As I held the lizard close to my face, it grew calm,
looking back at me from a corner of Being,
like a word not to be spoken.
I stared into its visible eye, catching
our forms deeper within the tiny iris.

I thought then how easy it would be
to disappear, to change shape, to allow
the atom its common song . . .

If only.

IMPERMANENCE

those perfect lips
the tongue of course
hidden

be patient, darling . . .
we have all the time
in the world

where she once moved
in the vacant room
a lingering grace

DAWN

first light
sycamore naked
in the stream

clouds building
out of
emptiness

the great owl
paddles
silently home

WAKING THE DREAM

Driving south on highway 1 between Cambria and Cayucos, California, I see a face hovering in a field. A leprechaun? An angel? No, it's only a tree stump. Often I see shadows trailing just beyond my focus, peripheral, elusive. And yet, what do I really see? I have driven a familiar road for years without noticing a certain old house tucked back in the trees, and to be surprised and appalled by all those miles driven in sleep. Driving south again, this time on highway 101 a few miles north of San Luis Obispo, suddenly I see something moving on the green slopes, turning its thick neck as if emerging from a world utterly its own. The incongruity of what I think I see wakes me, for a moment. (I have a sneaky suspicion that that animal uses more of its brain than I do mine; which would explain why it is real and so often I am not.) It ignores me, as I zip by. And it is as if these words pop to life from bubbles of laughter. . .

> *just cruising along*
> *with the common herd—*
> *cow steps out of the billboard*

STORM

waking in thunder
that immeasurable
pause

lying in bed
and the room's
soft edges

distant rain
approaching
dawn light

MOUNTAIN HAIKU

gusty morning
clouds trailing ridge
ragged hawk

climbing the trail
mist and man
for nothing

excited boy
his hands overflowing
salamanders

high ridge
and the blowing mist
manzanita aglow

unreasonable joy
one foot in front
of the other

DRIFTER

old truck
open road
moon on the dashboard

black liquid
through a sieve of stars —
frog swimming backwards

morning dew
honeysuckle juice
and a lucky tongue

HOMELESS

suddenly . . .
over my shoulder
a man who isn't there

coffee pot
rusting in the dunes—
a bird's quizzical glance

old newspapers
pressed over high grasses—
a bottle neck-deep in sand

a man approaches
with his open hand—
asking for work

come back at noon,
I tell him—I'll have
something for you then

watching the street people:
his form dissolves
among forms

charred wood
scattered glass—
words still hovering

the old fellow returns
with his one good eye—
staggering

don't mind me
he grins—
I'm a veteran

SALT OF THE EARTH

salt of the earth
knowing when to laugh
in any language

Working in the fields beside people whose words I did not understand, I sought my native place, my plain song. Breaking bread with killers, addicts, lunatics and thieves, I first tasted the solitude of our common distance. Our seedlings were stunted in the dust, and yet wickedly alive, all things human and divine warring within us. I was watching and listening as if my life depended on it, knowing the hunger that sustains us will betray us in the end—the human heart keeping time in hemispheres of blood.

picking grapes . . .
beside me, and just like me,
another stranger

TWO FOR SUMMER

1.

Waiting. I would learn to act.
I would learn to love.

Waiting. I would endure.
I would sing loudly.

Waiting. I would stop writing.
Go fishing without a hook,
in a river that has no banks.

2.

Once, on a stormy day, sunlight
suddenly burst upon the green fields,
and the children shouted joyously,
"Look! the devil's beatin' his wife!"
And as Grandma, flour up to her elbows,
leaned across the wood-stove,
a rainbow blossomed in the glistening corn.

ONE JUMPS FREE

still lake—
expanding circles remark
the loon's sudden presence

deserted beach—
driftwood's dull sheen
in the thick fog

after the flood
the apple tree
is an island

all my life
looking out of windows—
phases of the moon

kind thoughts . . .
even the willow
has a soft heart

returning home . . .
fooled again into waving
at the scarecrow

moonlit pond . . .
the poet's cough
silences the frogs

early spring . . .
floating into the tulip cup
a flake of snow

winter rains—
a clear lake manifested
beside the green hills

dark forest . . .
tiny shoots risen
in last year's leaves

Indian summer . . .
the sleeping dog growls deeply
in a cloud of gnats

a flower rescued
from the curbside drain—
the blossom of her smile

strong wind
the last leaf
releases

how serenely
he greets the blowing snow—
faded blue Buddha

stepping outside
into the frosty air—
first star, same old wish

DEAD MAN TALKING

Do not begrudge me your home.
All the walls have come down for me,
and now nothing stands between us,
not even a thought.

AN ENTITY'S LAMENT

Where experience and fantasy meet,
there am I,
blinded as much by truth as by fiction.

OLD SOUL

suddenly old
the heart speaks again
childhood

transparent years
the senses
thinned

winter moon
white stone
on a dark hill

PRISONER

Put on like skin, taut,
over a bubble of fire,
the real scribe hides like a shaman
whispering through a cauldron of bones.

Listening, I grope
for the song he sings in me.

I believe that one day
both of us will escape.

RIVER

The song flowed forth on the river's surge,
but somehow the sense of it all,
the feel of it upon my flesh,
kept receding.

I love the currents by which I shall never return.
They will wash me clean of desire and art.

I will float away.

Away.

MANTRA

what *you* do not say
to the silence
repeating it
until the silence
answers

LIZARD

meditating in the sun –
lizard's awakening

Skittering out from beneath the loose boards
to wonder at this lump of flesh basking in sunlight.
Opening my eyes, I catch him staring at me
from his perch on a cinder-block wall. I study him
closely in his peculiar aspects of humanity:
the thin fingers, the lidded eyes, the face, intent
and curious – a face emerged from the void
in dancing molecules of light, perfectly itself in
a world of mirrors, forming in each moment
the mysterious topography of presence.

eye to eye,
our real kinship
eluding us

The lizard was studying the *known*, while I
focused on the *unknown*. Between us, and
sustaining us, face to face, the *unknowable.*

curious lizard . . .
rejecting with such quickness
my still, human hand

THE ARTIST

The palette almost empty,
she seeks what she has sought all along—
the formless, the form

III
THE BREATH OF THINGS
LIGHTLY BORNE

STILL LIFE

He smiles.
According to the quantum modality
he has collapsed this moment,
and in effect invented a world,
which, so invented,
reflects back to him
the perception and sensibility
of his own *personal* dream,
piece by piece
in the piecemeal eternity.

It may be, he thinks.
Or it may not be. . .

He thinks of all the years of his life,
as though they were the unpublished chapters
of a stranger's autobiography,
interesting but not pertinent to his time.

He smiles, thinking . . .
so ghastly, so beautiful, and . . .
(dare he think it?)
divine.

ALONG THE SOUTHERN PACIFIC

A metal structure, long abandoned,
leans dangerously on its stilts, rust like pollen,
the dust of years. White flowers shine
in the brush, refusing to be anonymous.
Black stumps in the bayou, the far-seeing gulf,
white herons and willows, a pool of rotting fish.
Gravestones beside an industrial waste,
simple white crosses adorned with flowers.
A chemical plant, white smoke billowing.
Unpainted, washed-out houses,
sagging on their foundations.
Two dogs frisk in the desperate meadow.

VOICE

My words catch in my throat. . .
All the years trying to explain the spirit's wishing,
this wishing tree, dropping seeds foolishly
upon the common ground, this life,
uprooted, carried for meaningless distances
groaning in thirst.

Is there a center to this emptiness,
a place where all the nonsense becomes relevant?
Will I ever see anyone as they are? Will anyone ever see me?

Sometimes truth is bearable. It proves its worth.
The delusions drift apart, and the sun bursts
through the seams. . .

The heart is alone –
in every conversation the unspoken
haunting the fragile distance of the unspeakable,
voice falling back upon silence.

It strikes me that every seed must surrender,
crack open and die, into life.

ETHIC

I shave in the muted yellow light of responsibility,
preparing myself for the solitude and heartbreak
poised on the edge of a day.

I may not find sufficient reason, but I will continue.
That which I pursue may not bring me joy,
but it will sustain me.

I will take my work into my hands,
and made a few dollars wiser in the scarred afternoon,
I will earn the keeping of my life and death.

HOLY TERROR

I still recall that first blind night
enlightened by a mortal thought,
the terror of my extinction, the dread of loss,
the loves lost in black infinity.
Particularly the thought of my Mother's death.
Such horror to realize she would one day leave me.
I lay in the spinning dark, a child of alarm
and tender terror, the being of being human
raging in my veins.

Nothing would ever be the same;
not Christmas or young kisses;
not the journey or the dream of home.
Suffering, too, took on the air of insignificance,
dream-like as if belonging to another.

Terror and sadness shine in a man's bones,
the inexplicable hewn in the plodding days . . .
and sometimes, sculpted out of idiot longing,
arrives the fine bright angel of an open heart.

JUST THIS

When I read sad and ancient poems
I feel how in every detail
time sends the subtle transformations
which end at our beginning,
our lives beyond us as we rush away
thinking we know our heart's desire.
There are no perfect words for this living.
There is nothing new nor old.
Here it is, just this, just now,
and just so.

Once I played with a child
who did not question my motives, my form of play,
and even the air was music.

I felt myself standing in the center of moments,
the best of me silent and engaged.

TIME

Clouds drift and tear.
Stepping higher, breathing harder,
I focus on the climb.

From here I see the gentle sprawl of the town,
the details of the heart stretched taut
against a background of mysterious echo.
The air whispers like a lover saying farewell,
freedom, compassion.

There must be a height
from which everything is found,
and the life knows once again
that sense of wonder and awe.

As if we were in this moment complete;
as if time were nothing after all.

MY DAUGHTER READING THE TAO

The confidence born of failure. . .
Any door will do, walk through it
and believe – the sky trembles
at the edge of a leaf.

A child's amazing grace
succumbs to the mind's hopeless carvings,
and the hermit's uncarved block
becomes a mask for the agony of creation.

Winnie The Pooh tumbles over a hill
among butterflies and daffodils,
and is not hurt, and does not complain.

We grieve the loss of our natural step
through the fragrant glade. . .
But there is a confidence born of failure.

Any door will do,
walk through it and believe.

MY FLORIDA

Across the wide, flat field, green in perfect light, a roam of cows graze with their familiars, the unobtrusive white heron, skipping deftly between bug and hoof . . .and the bloated sky floats serenely in the elliptic eye. Pine and palmetto, distant, isolate and ethereal, glisten with dew—and the storm comes creeping from the south. The day begins in the humid intensity of sunlight, light through a prism, light held aloft and sparkling, and ends with the quick strike of lightning and the blast of thunder, the dark sky shattered by the intimacy of light. The power often fails. . .

A solitary man scribbles in a notebook—Where is my Florida? Where is my life? He amuses himself, pulling titles out of the air: *The One Percent Exception; Flatulence and the Firefly; The Glory of Corpses.* Sometimes the sky is an intricate mass of color running slowly toward the sea. There is never a still life. There are lemon trees, and grapefruit, and of course the ubiquitous orange and pine. When the blossoms open, the incense of citrus and sap pervades the blanket of air with an almost promiscuous penetration—one can scarcely breathe!

A white road disappears among orange trees—pure white sand and deep leathery green. The sky is big—for the land is flat—and the sea surrounds this nub of earth, laughing storms and distance, as if we were unwitting sailors, dumbstruck and adrift in our patchwork humanity.

Increasing marshland to the south, until the glades become ever-present and vast—alligators and manatees, weird-looking bugs, and the faithful crow . . . Life, burgeoning life, dancing in the reeds. The vultures are pure black and agile, like a crow on steroids, only not so much the dreamer. They look around as they tear and feast.

The Peace River, the Calusahatchee, the Myakka, all tributaries, swamps and creeks are swollen. This has been a stormy summer. Solitary trees, isolated in the surge, have become islands, and stand gasping in the currents drift and plunge . . . Even the mosquitoes are drowning. But sometimes the air feels right, and the light glows with a warmth almost tactile, almost human. I am filled with empathy and shame.

Perhaps I should not look too far. Yucatan to the west, Colombia to the south, and the feeling I would sail, anonymous as color or a face . . . the proper temperature and the presupposing wind. But I am a man, not a boat. I swim toward myself among the splintered waves. The mangrove are woven to desultory stone, a labyrinth reserved for our feathered friends,

snakes and witches. The Gulf is green. When the river exceeds its path and
the adjacent trees are steeped, a dull, reddish, rust-colored tea lies upon the
saturated ground, smelling of decay.

The bald eagle can be seen at times, and a tiny red bird on the electric line
reminds me of a toy that, years ago, turned out to be a snake . . . Road kill
is everywhere: armadillos, turtles, raccoons . . . made this way, of course,
by the speed that killed them. And the innocence. People mow their lawns
between downpours.

I cannot find my Florida. I am here, *I think.*
Like everything else in my life . . . it is beyond me,
floating incognito in a nebulous dream,
as if waiting to be discovered.

I forgot to mention the moon, the sea-faring moon
and the night sky that never sleeps.

FIRST PILLOW

Where will I lay this fat head,
this fat head I've beaten against walls,
spurting the blood of passion
into a sieve? this fat head
I call my life, flaunting
the headdress of my own
survival?

Dark life,
dragged kicking and screaming
into the light—this is my first pillow.

FLIGHT FROM LOS ANGELES

Shooting through the sky at thirty thousand feet . . .
and death is a living presence, telling me who I have become.
Behind me a little girl sings softly a sweet melody;
in front of me an Indian family begin to eat
the rice they have brought for sustenance on this budget flight.
The air is filled with the ancient musty pungency of curry.
At this moment we are jetting across the sky
as if the entire cosmos were our very own. Below us,
a sea of white clouds soft enough to dream in.
It is good to know where your life is;
to know you are not in control.
The horizon is vast and beautiful,
the color of a ripe peach.

DUALITY

Two streams, parallel and anonymous,
two voices, soft and troubled,
two lives, one silent and one proud,
fall, perpetually, toward the burning sea.
I live the ebb and flow, yes and no,
pleasure and pain, my life a dream
I do not own, my death equally void.
Forgive me, then, for having nothing
to show you – no proof, nor lasting gift.
But from somewhere a river of love
flows between us, singular and free.

PATH

Rising once again in unwilled opposition
to my own spirituality or lack thereof,
the sky with all its sorcery becomes
a perfect representation of the absence
and confusion I live and breathe
in this furtive and finite journey between beliefs,
smart enough to know what I believe
but too dumb to believe what I know:
that beautiful life, torturing this pittance.

MOON CHILD

In love with the moon,
she begins to sing the beauty of her perception.
In truth, it isn't the beauty that pleases her.
It is the magnificence of the mystery
she herself inhabits, beyond words or meaning;
as if the moon were something she intuited
in the native explication of Being.

She punches me on the arm to look closer
behind the pines on the hill – such a moon!
Leaning into the shadows, she sighs
like a satisfied woman whose lover
will never be identified.

CROSSING TEXAS IN MOONLIGHT

This land, once stolen by murder and greed,
a hundred years removed, is still unused
and uninhabited—no windmills,
no solar collectors, no cultivated fields;
only the lonesome chaparral, burning
in the shade-less distance.

This train travels in time,
my own dark history rising
from the iron wheels, and driving me
onwards, suspended between beliefs.

A young Kiowa stands on a dark mesa
beneath a billion stars, and dreams of horses and women,
years of good hunting, the fulfillment of his heart.
The wind and the distance answer—
an approaching train of alien desires
as strong and unreasonable as his own.

THE TAO OF WALKING
AND DREAMING

Breathe in, breathe out. Eat, then wash your bowl.
But anger sends me into the wilderness blind,
and a strong and stupid world undermines
the will to survive, and such a will, subverted,
sometimes wants to die. Or seek life elsewhere.
Life without flavor; vitamins of the absurd.
Talking mannequins, lies and lies.
And then to struggle toward the trail,
where the Spanish moss, palm and oak,
arc the painted sky – an alcove of reflection,
beautiful enough to be believed, one's questions
walking hand in hand with the answer,
sensual and divine.

Little creatures scurry in the undergrowth,
and, turning, you catch the trail of a shadow,
disappearing underground or into the sky.
To be alive is to be responsible. It is a voice
found in wild moments of good sense;
as the tree stands to the houses of song
in forbearance and with an aspect,
one might say, of listening.

Less angry, I entered no-place;
and I was grateful for the nothing
that was happening all around me.

THE LIFE OF THIS WORLD

Where darkness falls onto pools of light
and the wind drives the trees like stubborn cattle,
there's only mystery, a man and woman
looking beyond the trees
toward something that cannot be told.

How can we reach each other?
How can we not? Her lips brush mine
with the sweetness of the known.

She danced through my life
with such grace and beauty,
my heart was its own breaking.

Her lips had no more need of hunger.
Her song was a bird perched
within impenetrable night,
content with its silence.
I wanted so badly to hear her sing.

The blue heron and the white heron
cross the silent marsh.
Do they trust the other's flight?
Do they know where they are going?

Desire is a mask, a dream.
The life of this world is not in this world.
We live, if we live at all,
inseparable, perfect, unseen.

LEAVING LOS ANGELES BY TRAIN

The sun is falling behind the hills in the city of angels,
the window stained with the dust of years.
A fast train, and this time, on time, sounds its plaintive warning
as we move stealthily toward what
we cannot see and do not know.

In the seat in front of me,
a child's toy is teaching the ABC's.
The little girl coos, smiling, still speaking
the language of the heart.

Her mother looks into the window where I am reflected.
She holds my gaze with her beauty, her strong
and delicate question, and her look is a challenge.

And I imagine us the way it could have been
if fate followed parallel roads to any sweet oblivion,
beyond all desire and loneliness,
and the limitations imposed by change.

But of course I have no answers, I look away—
and though I return my gaze, it is not met.

Mother proffers her ripe breast,
the stained window casting a perfect holograph,
and her baby girl suckles in the twilight,
both of them luminous and mutable,
living, as always, on the edge
of something forbidden.

IN DUST AND STARLIGHT

Dark hills beyond the shore, the world is asleep.
The dreamer lies awake in his bed, listening
to a train braking in San Luis Obispo, California;
slowing through town, picking up speed,
and rattling away toward the southern oblivion.
It is cold and foggy in the sleeping world.
A heart awake is a terrible thing,
like distance squeezed into a glove.

DESERT SONG

The Saguaro stand tall in isolate perfection.
Awake to the air, they have claimed their ground,
and represent themselves accordingly—their flesh
as faith and being, their being as time,
and their time, for all time, as *Now*.

These are old friends, these reverential strangers,
holding their arms aloft as if in praise.
Standing in such beautiful solitude
three hundred years slide gently away
like a sigh of release.

THE BREATH OF THINGS LIGHTLY BORNE

When I lifted into the luminous, unwilling,
alone and unsure, it was by terror and human will
that I returned to speak to the human being beside me.
I was again reminded of the great mystery
to which I was born; how the nights remain open
to translation and danger, and infinitely human. . .
She squeezed my hand and said she smelled jasmine
in the air—how strange, jasmine where none existed.
And the fragrance of the divine frightened her.

She held me fast and begged me not to leave her. . .
Humanness breathed into my ear the only love
I could understand, and yet I feared it:
to be held; to be somehow real.

But I had no world, only the breath of things
lightly borne – their distinguishable fragrances
left behind like solitude.

ABOUT THE AUTHOR

Kevin Hull is a writer and poet, and the editor and publisher of White Heron Press. His work has appeared in numerous journals, both here and abroad, and occasionally as limited edition chapbooks. His memoir, *Nameless Traveler*, chronicles much of his notorious past as well as his encounters with poetry and grace. At present he is writing a novel. *LEAVING BLUE MOUNTAINS* is his first full-length collection.

Originally from the Blue Ridge Mountains of Virginia, he lived for many years on California's beautiful central coast. He currently resides in southwest Florida.